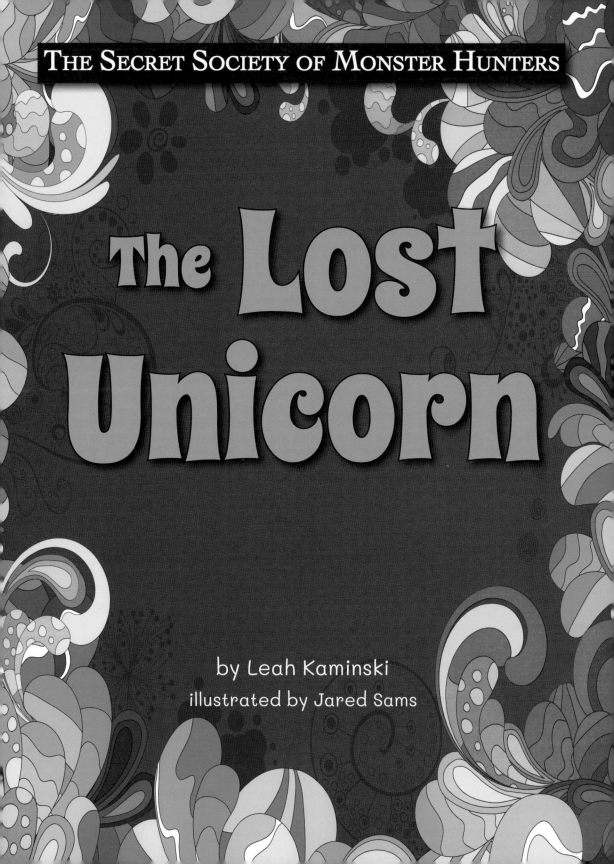

THE SECRET SOCIETY OF MONSTER HUNTERS

The Lost Unicorn

by Leah Kaminski

illustrated by Jared Sams

TORCH GRAPHIC PRESS

Published in the United States of America by Cherry Lake Publishing Group
Ann Arbor, Michigan
www.cherrylakepublishing.com

Reading Adviser: Marla Conn, MS, Ed., Literacy specialist, Read-Ability, Inc.

Book Design: Book Buddy Media

Photo Credits: page 1: ©Victor_Tongdee/iStock / Getty Images; page 9: ©uwdigitalcollections / Wikimedia; page 11: ©StockSmartStart / Shutterstock; page 11: ©xpixel / Shutterstock; page 13: ©Leunert / Pixabay; page 27: ©OpenClipart-Vectors / Pixabay; page 30: ©fdastudillo/iStock / Getty Images; page 30: ©CSA Images RF / Getty Images; background: ©suwanneeredhead/iStock / Getty Images (facts); background: ©OpenClipart-Vectors / Pixabay (lined paper); background: ©MarjanNo / Pixabay; background: ©Valeriya Belobragina / Shutterstock (sidebars)

Torch Graphic Press is an imprint of Cherry Lake Publishing Group.

Library of Congress Cataloging-in-Publication Data
Names: Kaminski, Leah, author. | Sams, Jared, illustrator.
Title: The lost unicorn / by Leah Kaminski ; illustrated by Jared Sams.
Description: Ann Arbor, Michigan : Torch Graphic Press, 2020. | Series: The Secret Society of Monster Hunters | Includes bibliographical references and index. | Audience: Ages 10-13. | Audience: Grades 4-6. | Summary: Jorge, Fiona, and Marcus travel to Woodstock in August 1969 to prevent the capture of a unicorn.
Identifiers: LCCN 2020017232 (print) | LCCN 2020017233 (ebook) | ISBN 9781534169425 (hardcover) | ISBN 9781534171107 (paperback) | ISBN 9781534172944 (pdf) | ISBN 9781534174788 (ebook)
Subjects: LCSH: Graphic novels. | CYAC: Graphic novels. | Unicorns—Fiction. | Time travel—Fiction. | Secret societies--Fiction. | Woodstock Festival (1969 : Bethel, N.Y.)—Fiction. | Woodstock (N.Y.)—History--20th century—Fiction.
Classification: LCC PZ7.7.K355 Lo 2020 (print) | LCC PZ7.7.K355 (ebook) | DDC 741.5/973—dc23
LC record available at https://lccn.loc.gov/2020017232
LC ebook record available at https://lccn.loc.gov/2020017233

Cherry Lake Publishing Group would like to acknowledge the work of the Partnership for 21st Century Learning, a Network of Battelle for Kids. Please visit http://www.battelleforkids.org/networks/p21 for more information.

Printed in the United States of America
Corporate Graphics

TABLE OF CONTENTS

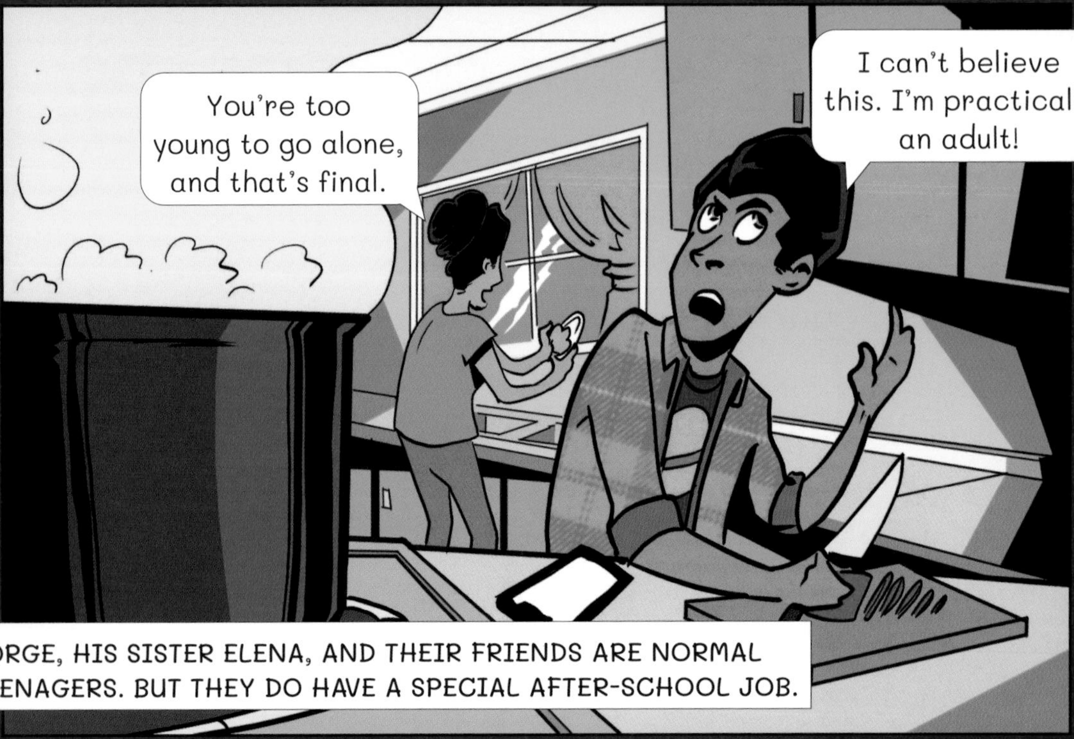
You're too young to go alone, and that's final.
I can't believe this. I'm practically an adult!
JORGE, HIS SISTER ELENA, AND THEIR FRIENDS ARE NORMAL TEENAGERS. BUT THEY DO HAVE A SPECIAL AFTER-SCHOOL JOB.

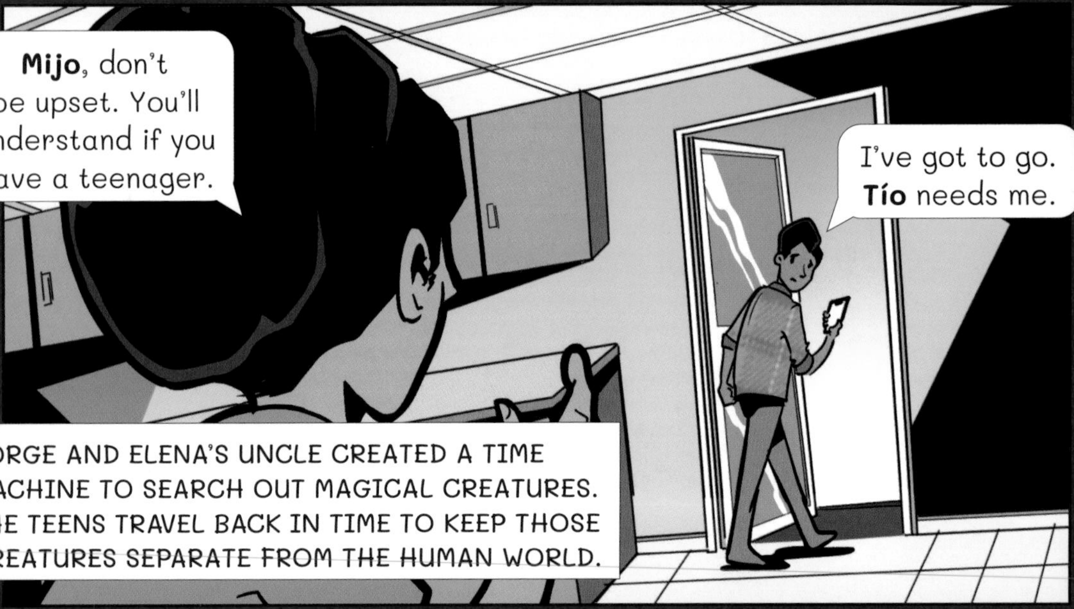
Mijo, don't be upset. You'll understand if you have a teenager.
I've got to go. **Tío** needs me.
JORGE AND ELENA'S UNCLE CREATED A TIME MACHINE TO SEARCH OUT MAGICAL CREATURES. THE TEENS TRAVEL BACK IN TIME TO KEEP THOSE CREATURES SEPARATE FROM THE HUMAN WORLD.

mijo: "my son" in Spanish

tío: "uncle" in Spanish

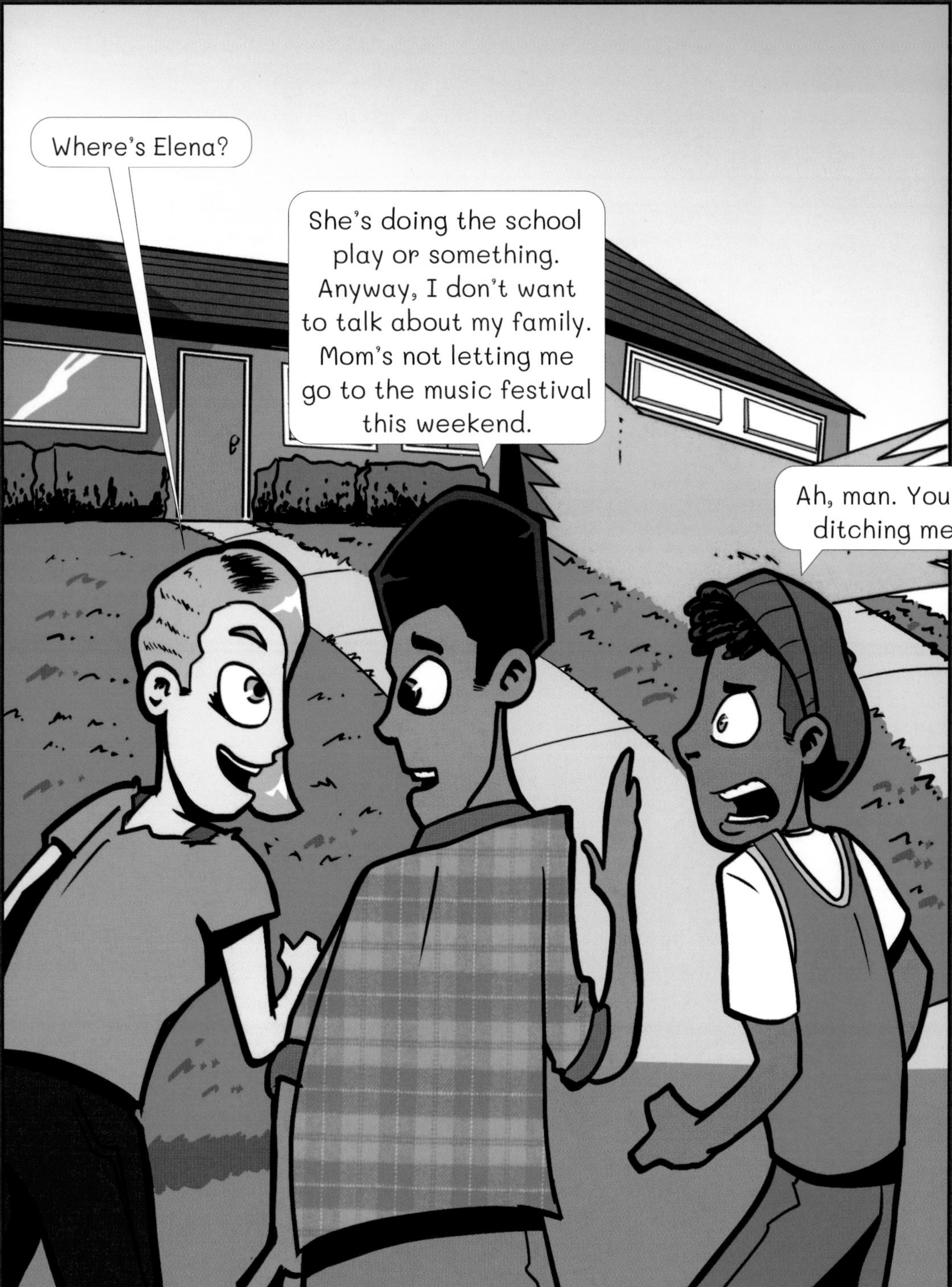
Where's Elena?
She's doing the school play or something. Anyway, I don't want to talk about my family. Mom's not letting me go to the music festival this weekend.
Ah, man. You're ditching me?

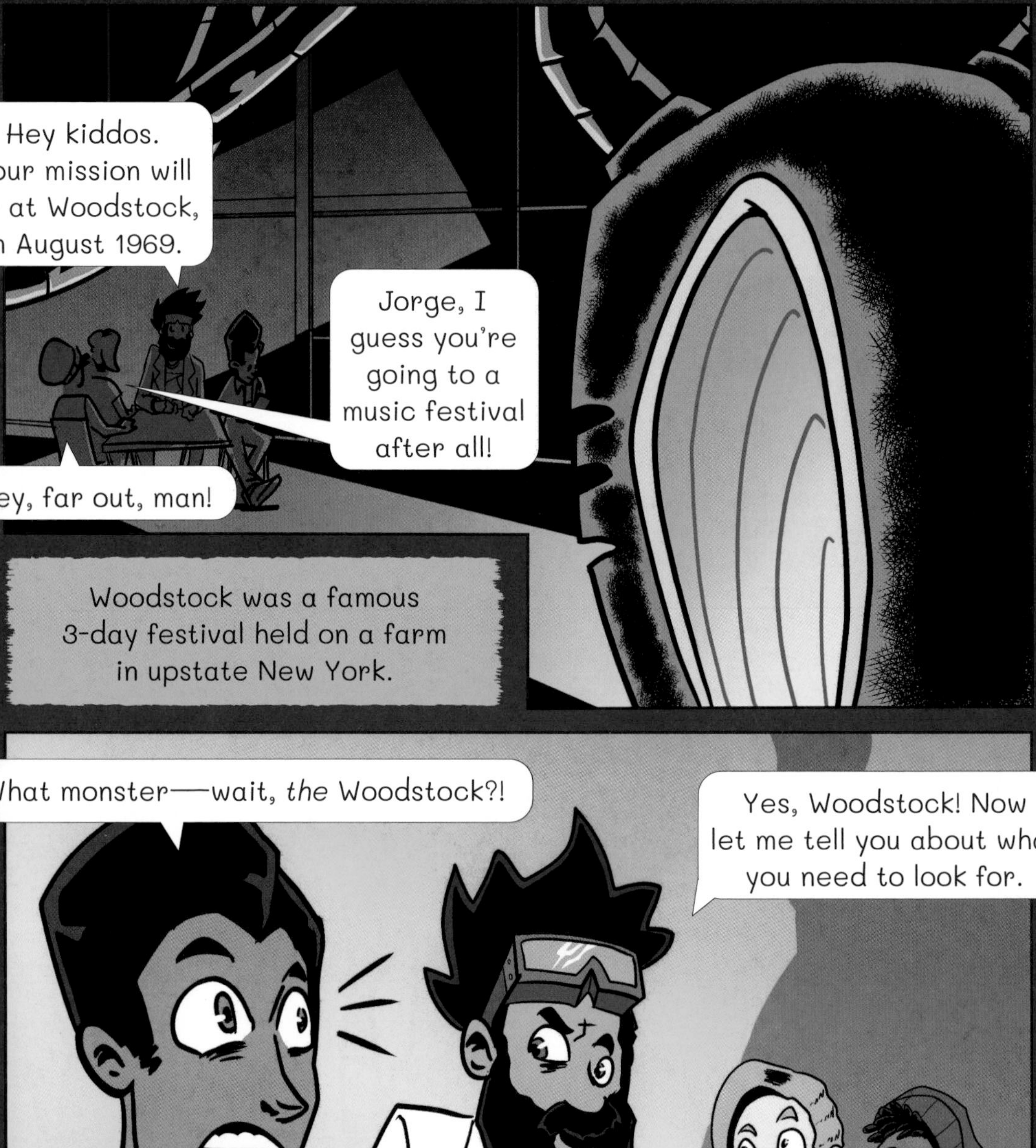
Hey kiddos. Your mission will be at Woodstock, in August 1969.
Jorge, I guess you're going to a music festival after all!
Hey, far out, man!
Woodstock was a famous 3-day festival held on a farm in upstate New York.
What monster—wait, *the* Woodstock?!
Yes, Woodstock! Now let me tell you about what you need to look for.

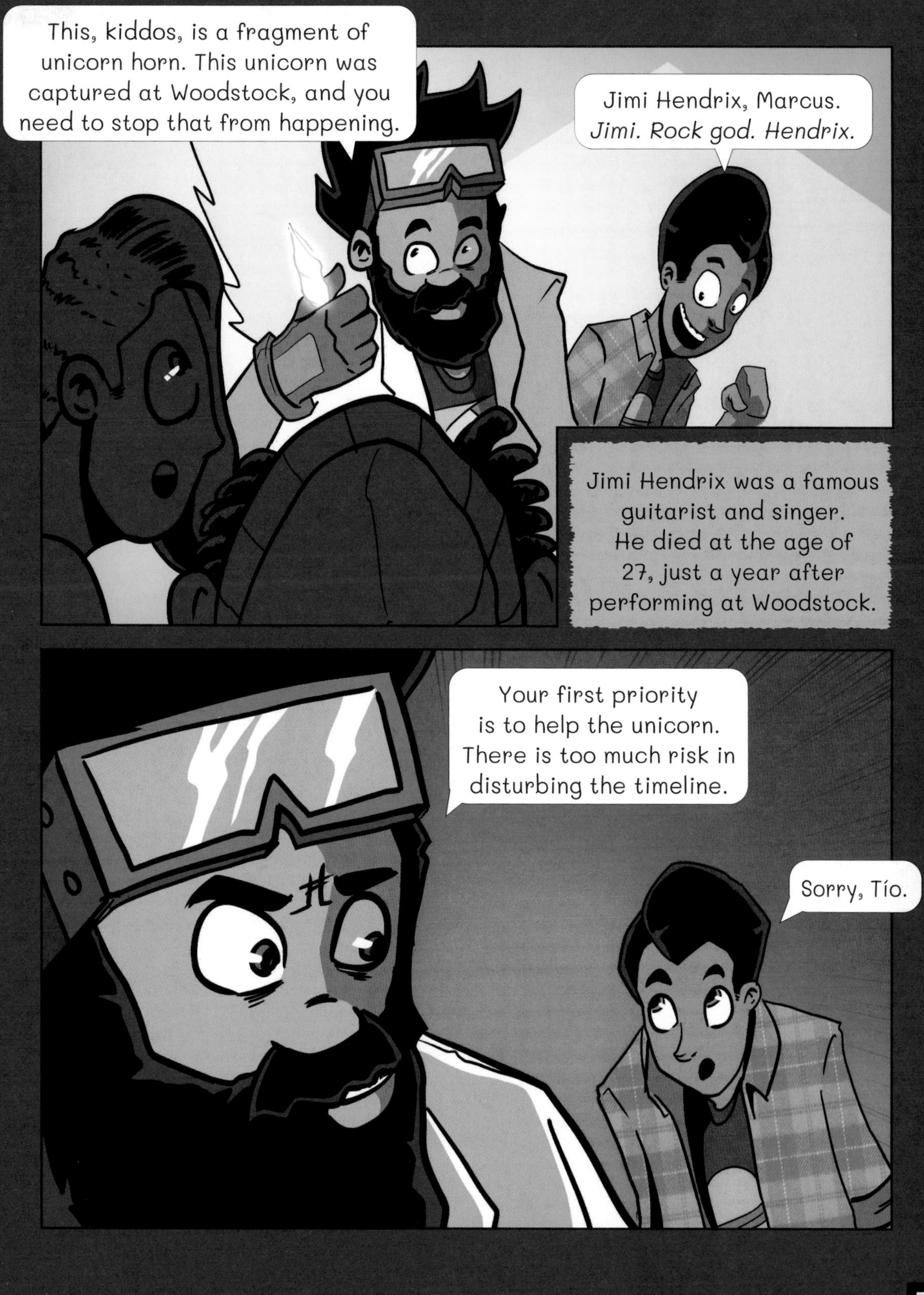

This, kiddos, is a fragment of unicorn horn. This unicorn was captured at Woodstock, and you need to stop that from happening.
Jimi Hendrix, Marcus. *Jimi. Rock god. Hendrix.*
Jimi Hendrix was a famous guitarist and singer. He died at the age of 27, just a year after performing at Woodstock.
Your first priority is to help the unicorn. There is too much risk in disturbing the timeline.
Sorry, Tío.

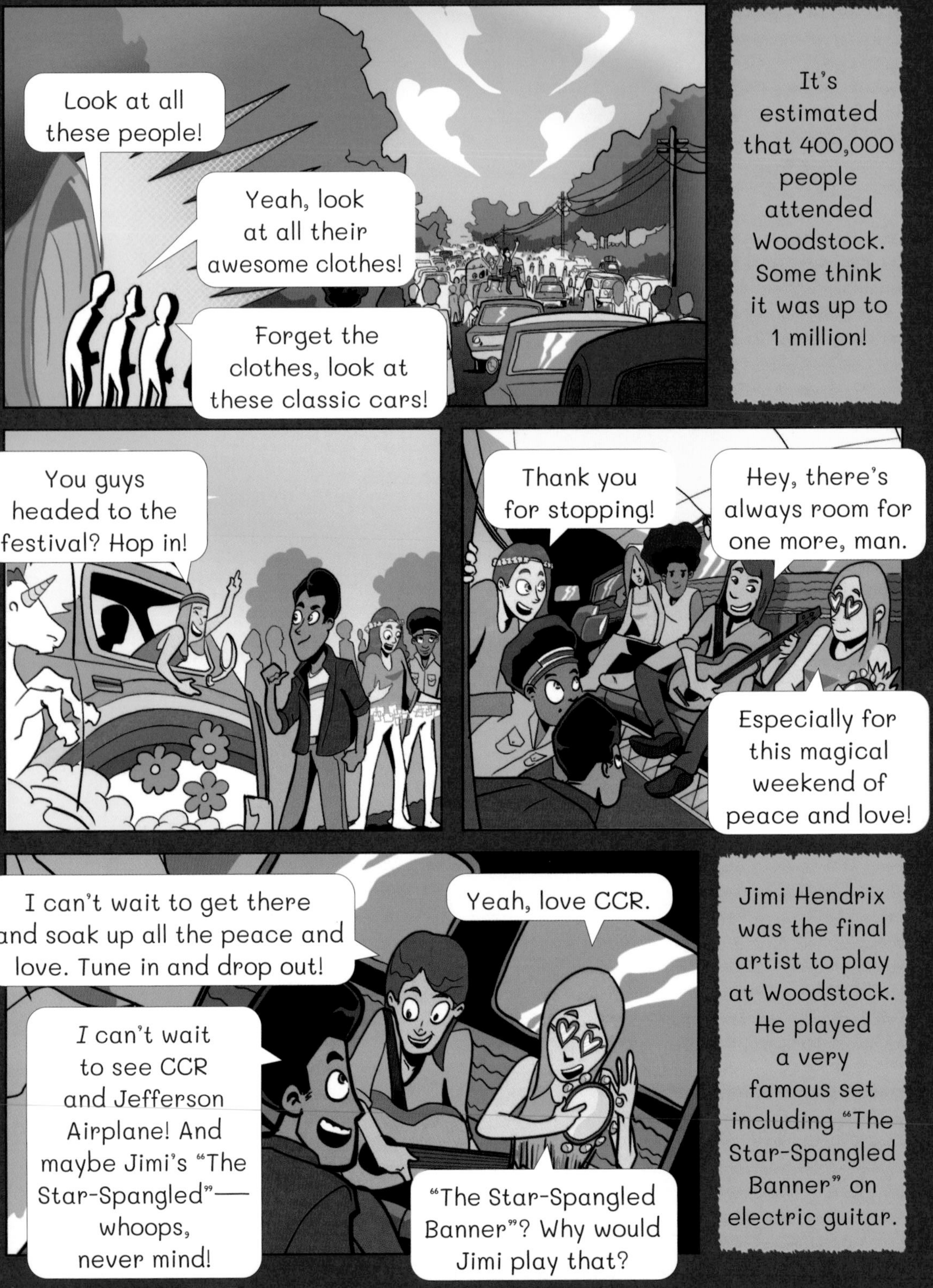
Look at all these people!
Yeah, look at all their awesome clothes!
Forget the clothes, look at these classic cars!
It's estimated that 400,000 people attended Woodstock. Some think it was up to 1 million!
You guys headed to the festival? Hop in!
Thank you for stopping!
Hey, there's always room for one more, man.
Especially for this magical weekend of peace and love!
I can't wait to get there and soak up all the peace and love. Tune in and drop out!
Yeah, love CCR.
I can't wait to see CCR and Jefferson Airplane! And maybe Jimi's "The Star-Spangled"— whoops, never mind!
"The Star-Spangled Banner"? Why would Jimi play that?
Jimi Hendrix was the final artist to play at Woodstock. He played a very famous set including "The Star-Spangled Banner" on electric guitar.

TIPS FOR THE DECADE

The 60s were a period of intense social and political change. Young people broke with the **conformist** culture of the 1950s and early 1960s

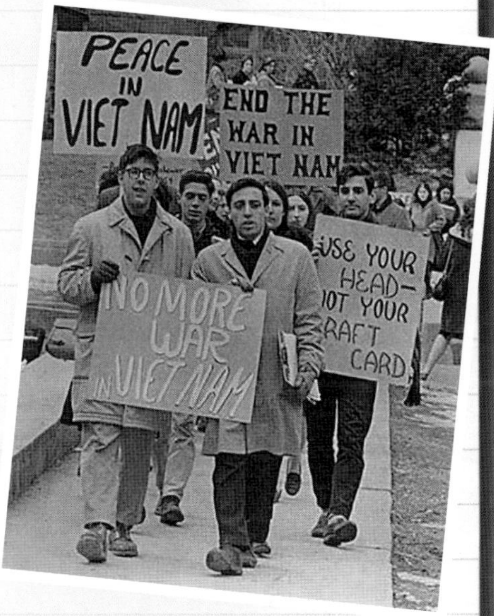
PEACE IN VIET NAM
END THE WAR IN VIET NAM
NO MORE WAR IN VIET NAM
USE YOUR HEAD- NOT YOUR DRAFT CARD

* Many "hippies" were political. Students took over colleges in protest of the **draft** and the Vietnam War.
* Multiple **civil rights** movements and the women's rights movement challenged long-standing racism and sexism.
* Music was a major influence on the culture. Folk music and rock music were more experimental than ever before.
* A lot of famous slang came from this decade. Something that was "righteous," "groovy," "a gas," or "far out" was good. Something not fun was a "drag" or a "bummer." If someone was "bugging out," they were panicking.

conformist: clinging to accepted rules and behaviors

draft: the act of selecting people for mandatory military service

civil rights: citizens' rights to freedom and equality

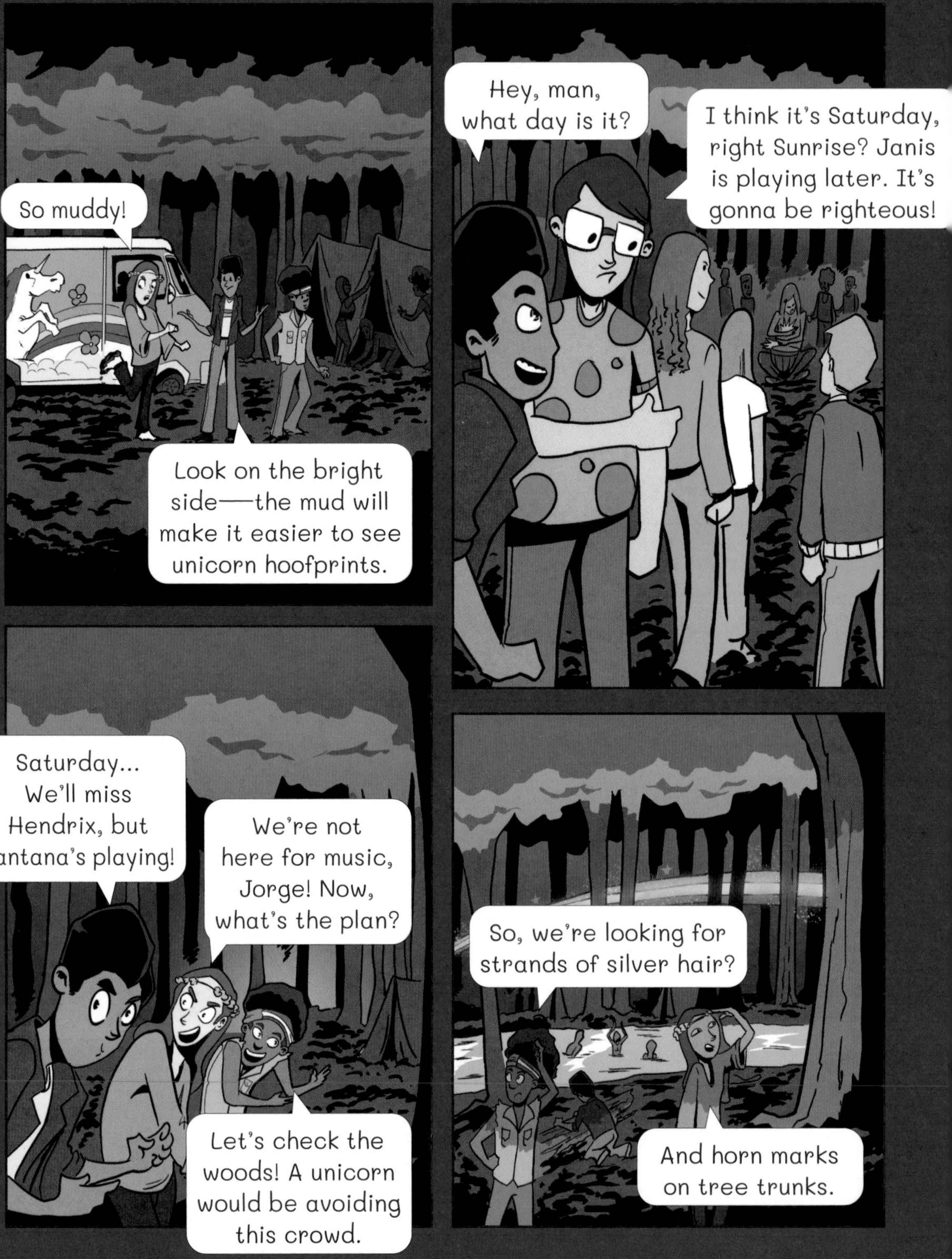
So muddy!
Look on the bright side—the mud will make it easier to see unicorn hoofprints.
Hey, man, what day is it?
I think it's Saturday, right Sunrise? Janis is playing later. It's gonna be righteous!
Saturday... We'll miss Hendrix, but Santana's playing!
We're not here for music, Jorge! Now, what's the plan?
Let's check the woods! A unicorn would be avoiding this crowd.
So, we're looking for strands of silver hair?
And horn marks on tree trunks.

PACKING LIST

In the late 1960s, many people were still wearing the **conservative** clothes of the 1950s and early 1960s. But styles were changing quickly.

* Young hippies wore loose, flowing clothes.

* Peasant dresses and shirts were popular for women.

* Men and women both wore bell-bottom jeans, headbands, and big sunglasses.

* Beads and leather were very popular.

* Other things people might carry around were leather wallets, Black Jack chewing gum, and portable radios.

conservative: traditional

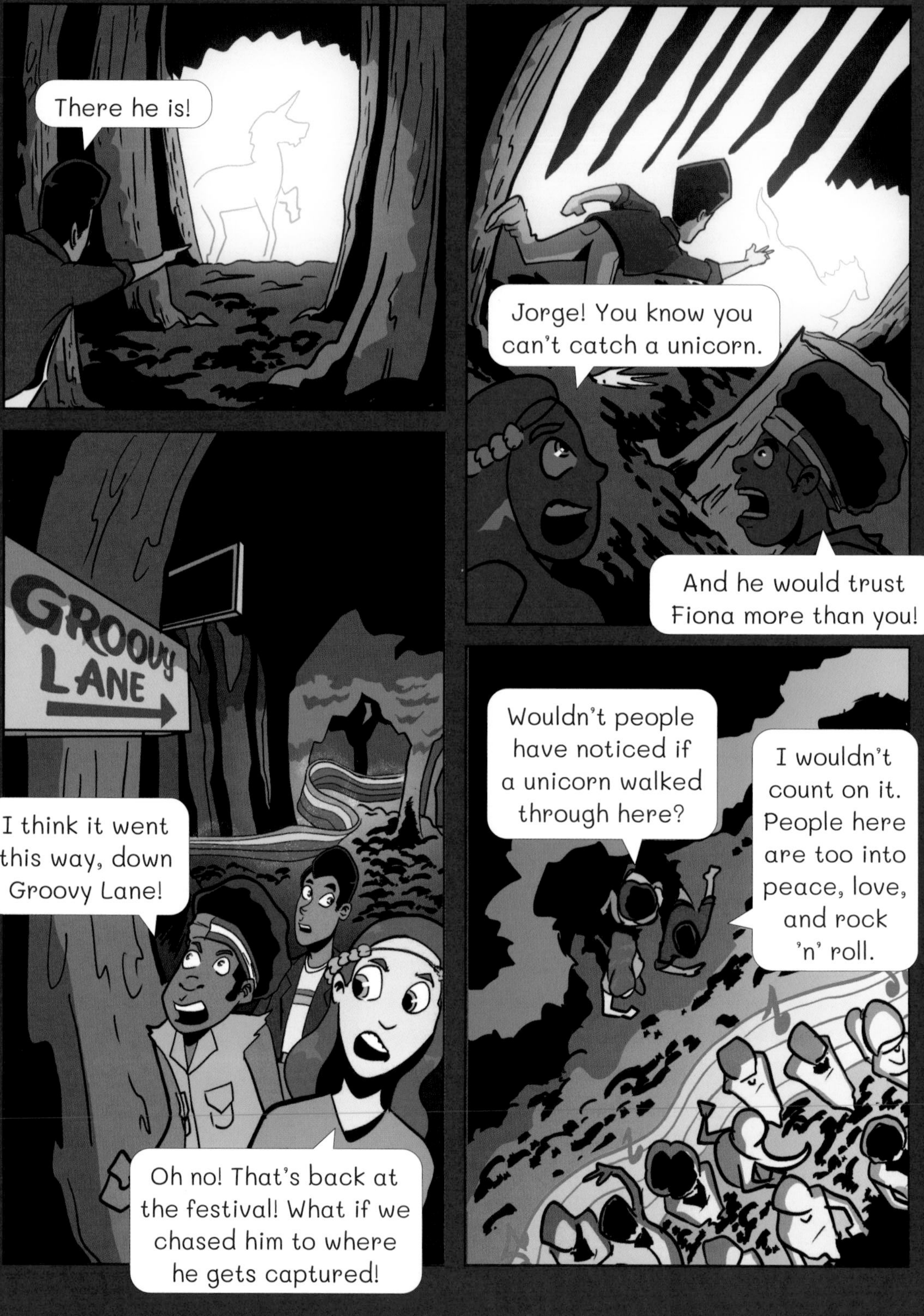
There he is!
Jorge! You know you can't catch a unicorn.
And he would trust Fiona more than you!
GROOVY LANE
I think it went this way, down Groovy Lane!
Oh no! That's back at the festival! What if we chased him to where he gets captured!
Wouldn't people have noticed if a unicorn walked through here?
I wouldn't count on it. People here are too into peace, love, and rock 'n' roll.

WHAT ARE UNICORNS?

Unicorns have shiny silvery-white hair and blue hooves. A unicorn's horn rises from its forehead in a spiral. The horns are magical. What else is magical about unicorns?

* They do not eat. Instead, they take energy from the sun. And they are **immortal**.
* Their horn can cure sickness and purify poisoned water.
* Unicorns would never attack, but they can defend themselves. Their horns are also weapons. They can be used like spears and are harder than diamonds.
* Unicorn blood is also magical. It's silver in color and anyone who drinks it becomes immortal.
* Unicorns know that there is purity in young people. The only people they are not afraid of are young women.

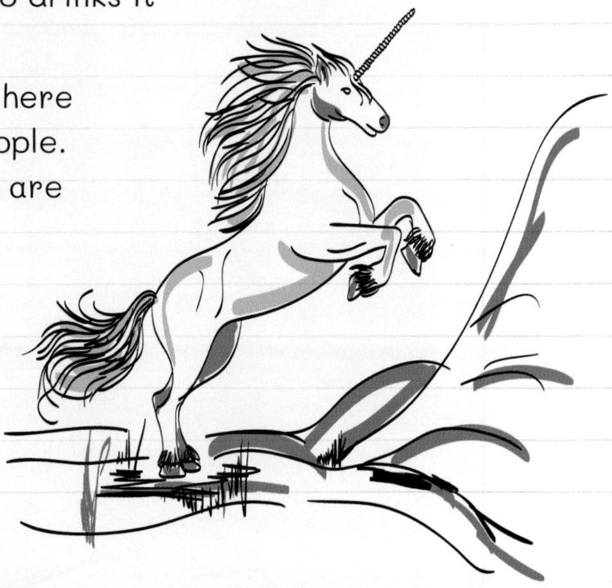

immortal: able to live forever

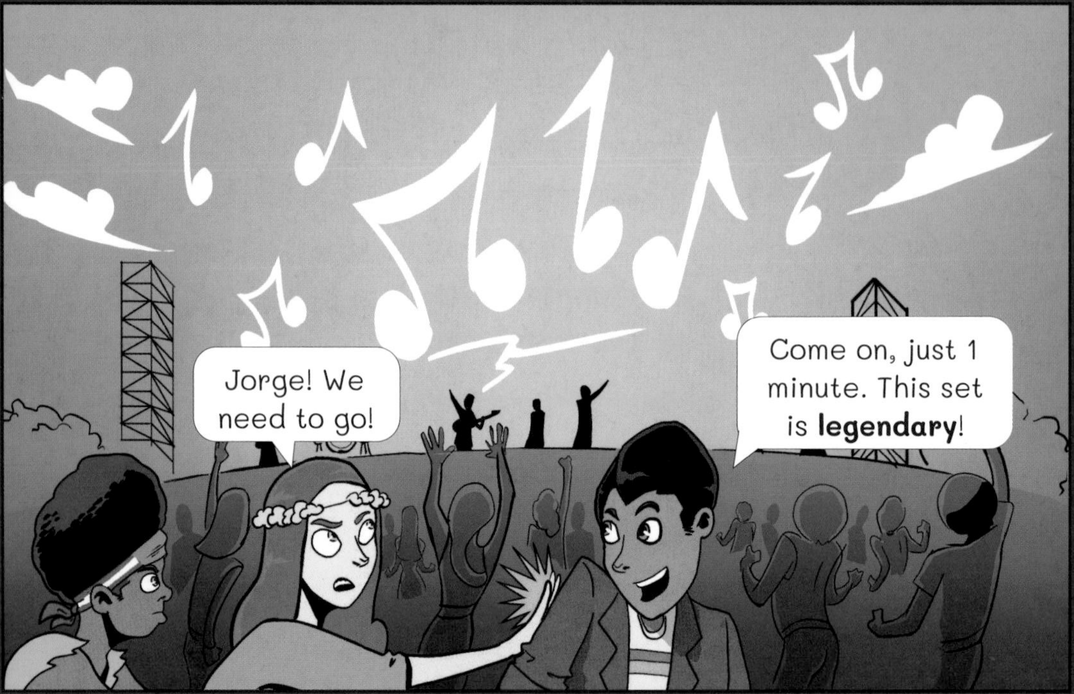
Jorge! We need to go!
Come on, just 1 minute. This set is **legendary**!

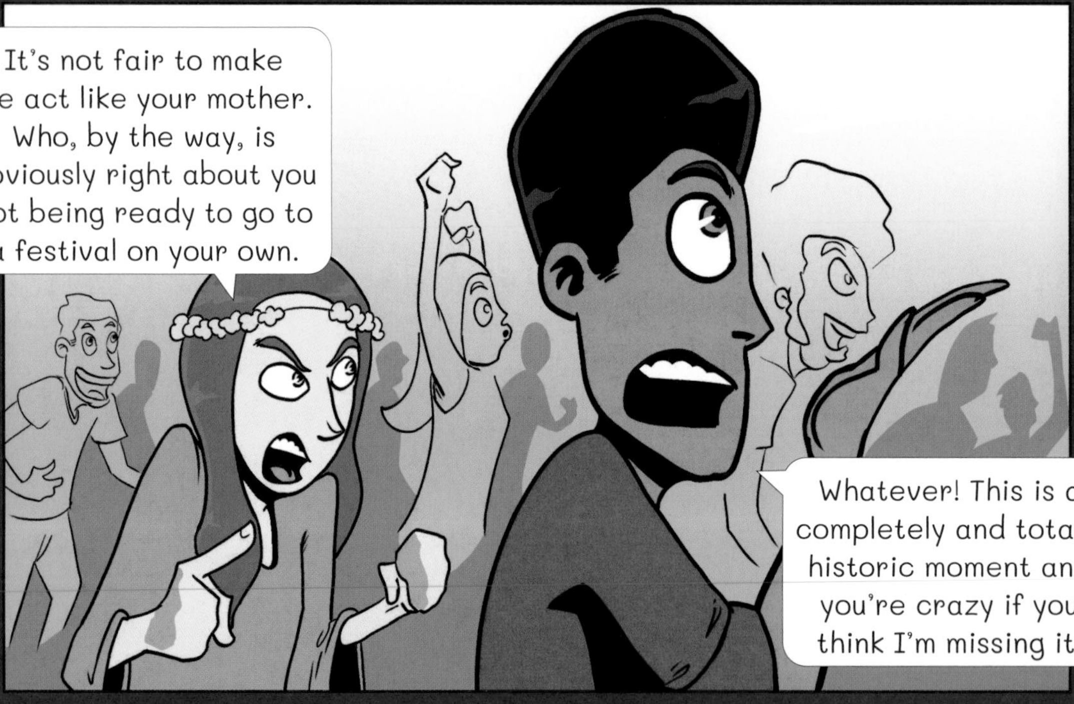
It's not fair to make me act like your mother. Who, by the way, is obviously right about you not being ready to go to a festival on your own.
Whatever! This is a completely and totally historic moment and you're crazy if you think I'm missing it!

legendary: famous

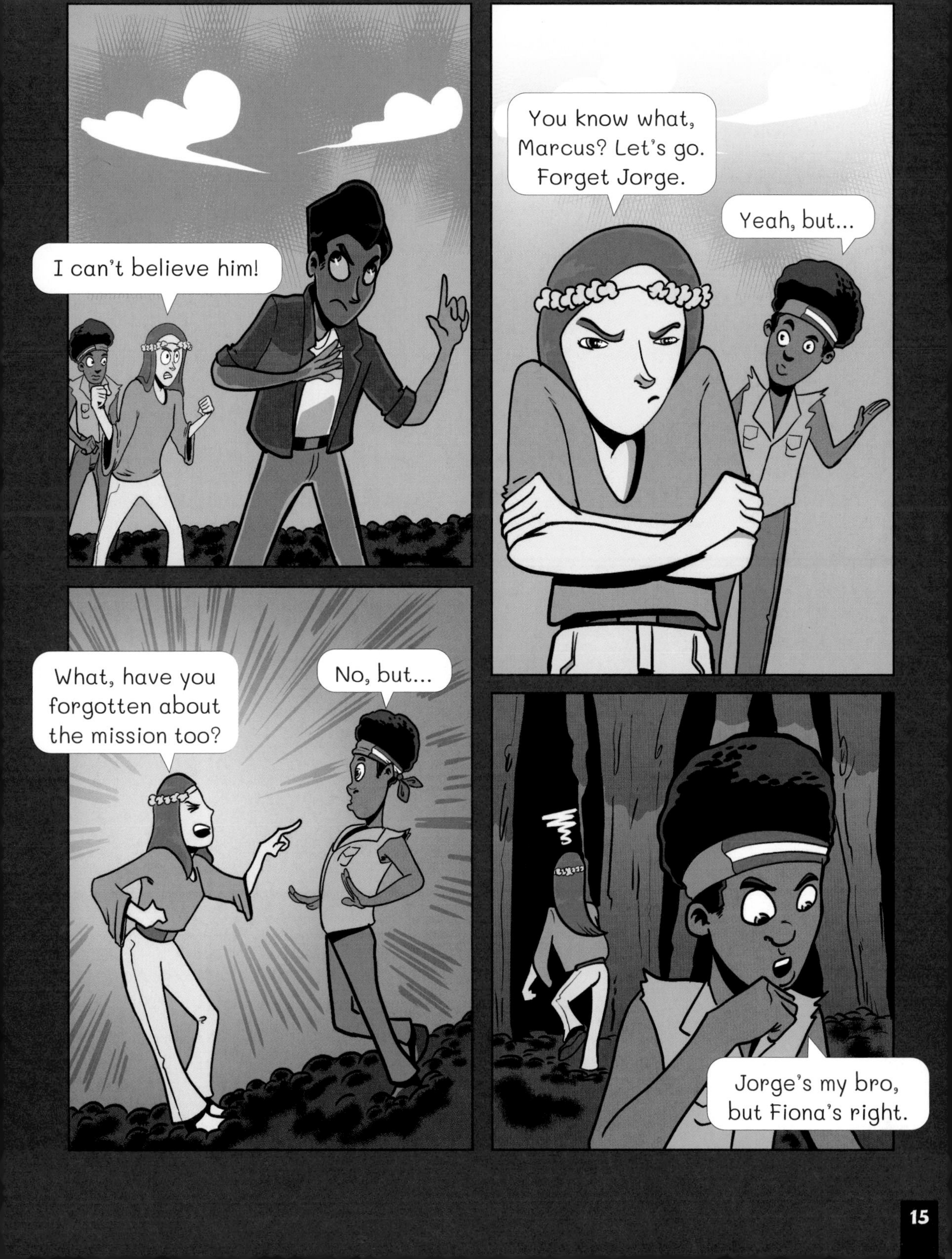
I can't believe him!
You know what, Marcus? Let's go. Forget Jorge.
Yeah, but...
What, have you forgotten about the mission too?
No, but...
Jorge's my bro, but Fiona's right.

You would think farm animals would be **agitated** from the concert...

...but they are so calm. This must mean the unicorn is near! I wonder where he is.

Sorry! I—

Marcus! I'm glad you're here. Keep watch outside!

agitated: in a state of heightened activity

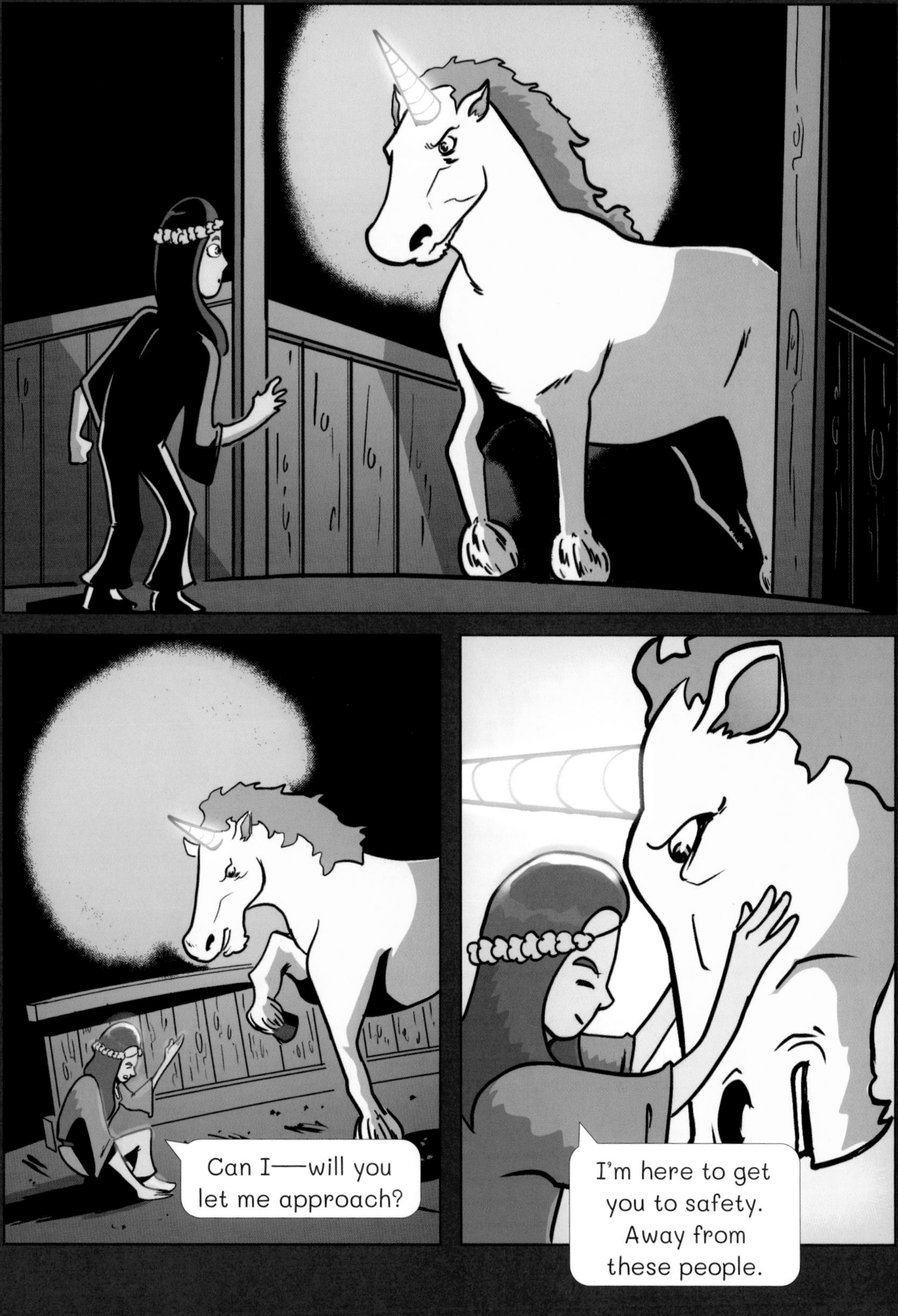

Can I—will you let me approach?
I'm here to get you to safety. Away from these people.

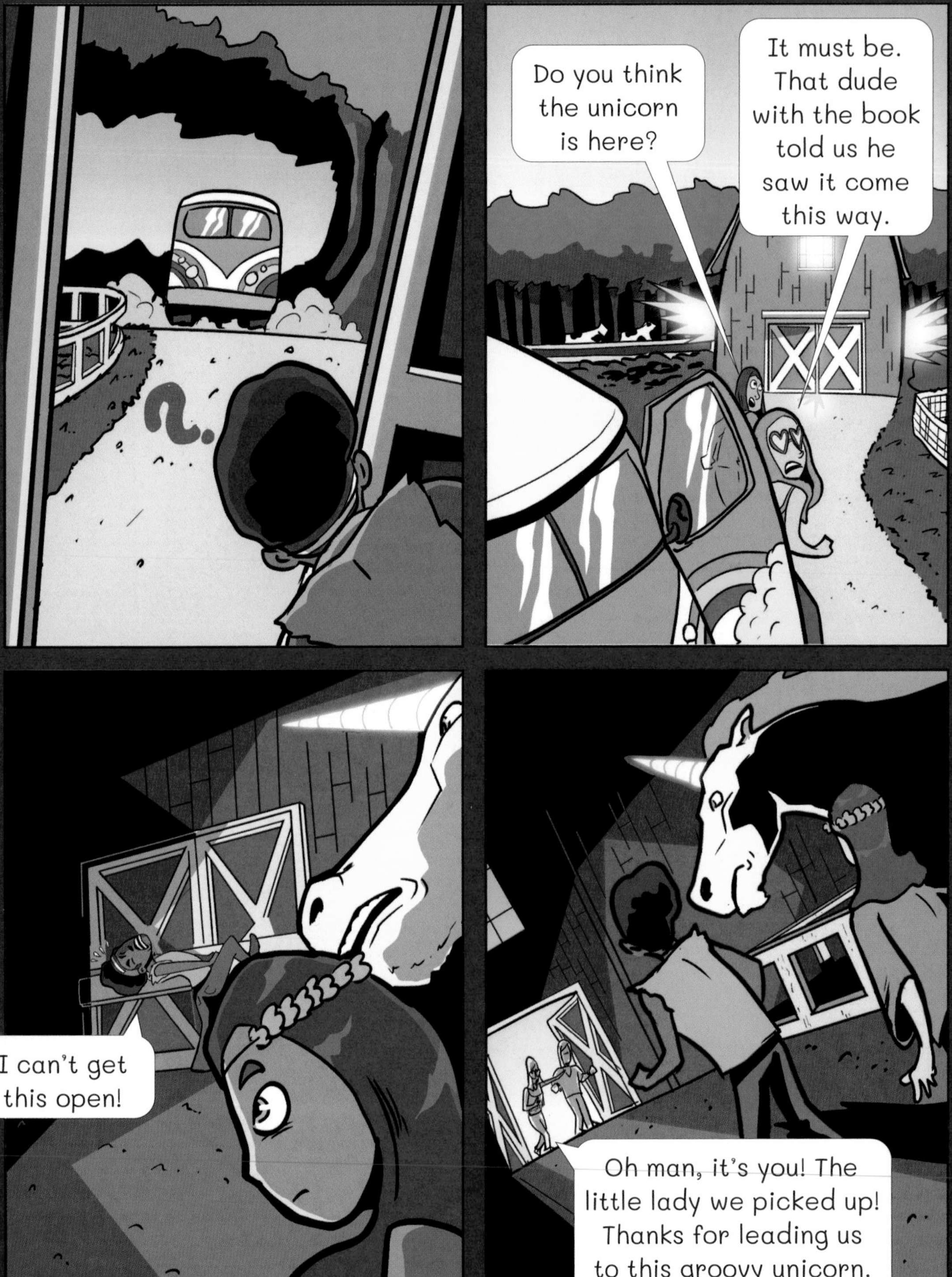
Do you think the unicorn is here?
It must be. That dude with the book told us he saw it come this way.
I can't get this open!
Oh man, it's you! The little lady we picked up! Thanks for leading us to this groovy unicorn. I guess everything happens for a reason!

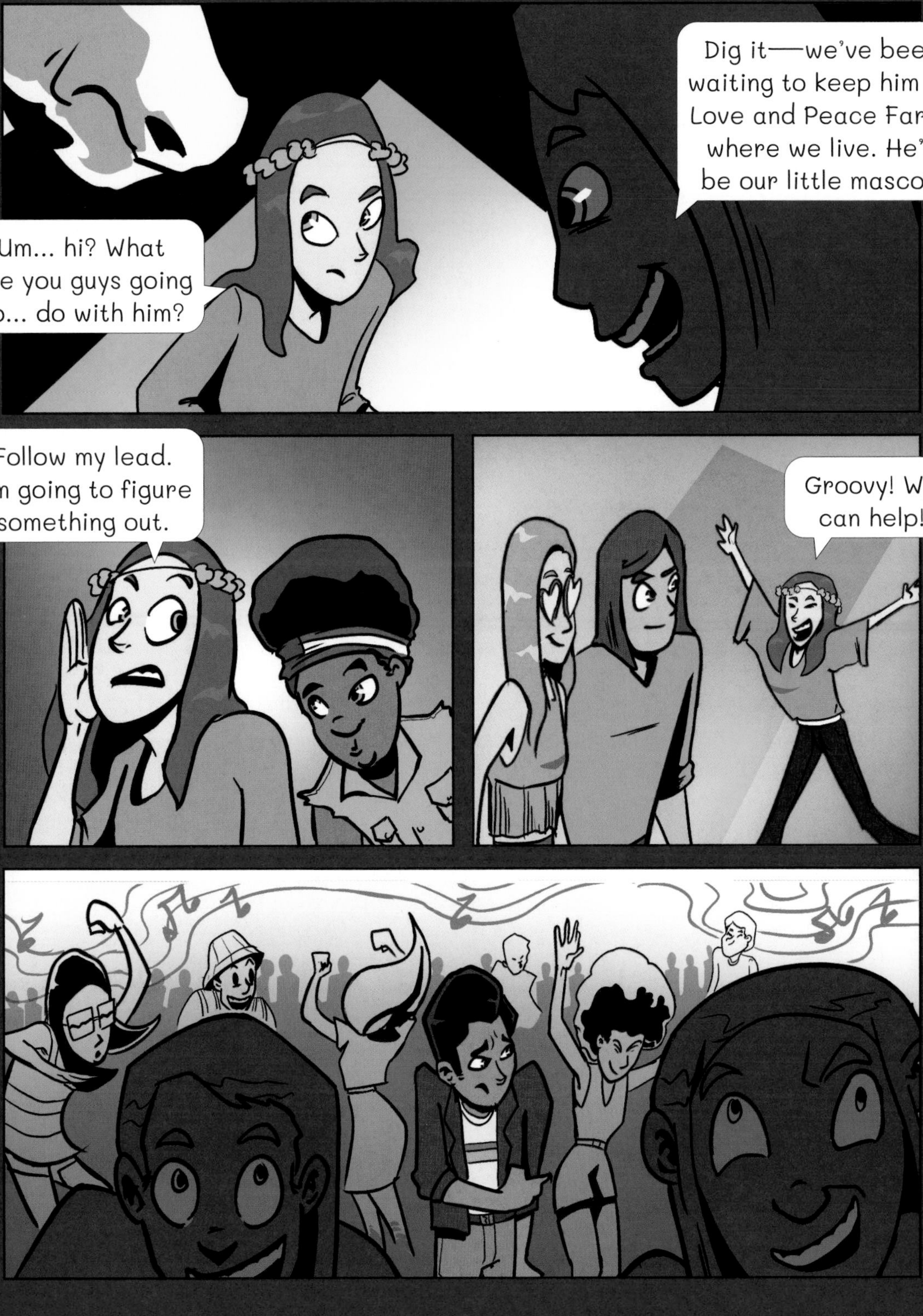
Dig it—we've been waiting to keep him on Love and Peace Farm, where we live. He'll be our little mascot!
Um... hi? What are you guys going to... do with him?
Follow my lead. I'm going to figure something out.
Groovy! We can help!

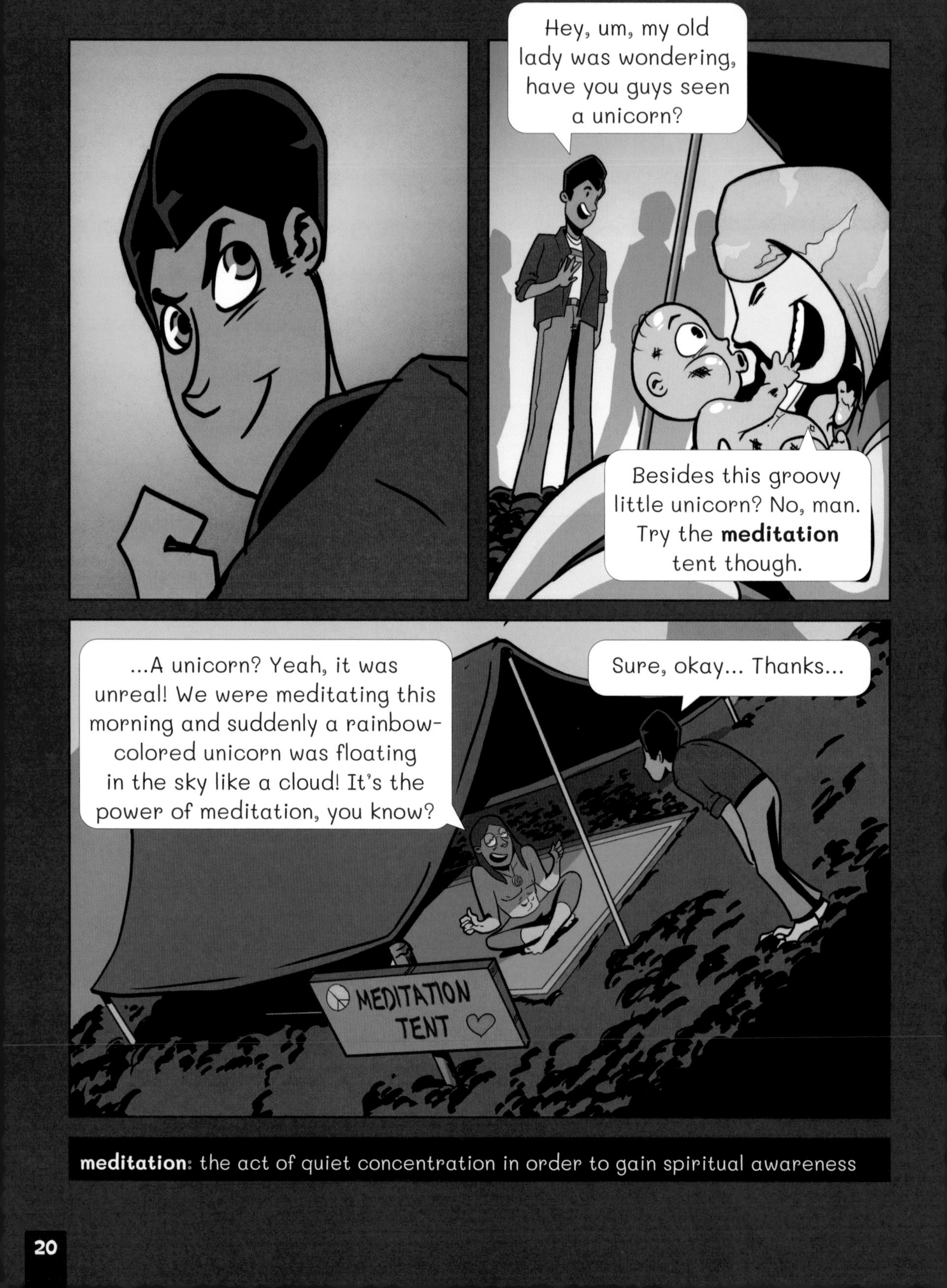
Hey, um, my old lady was wondering, have you guys seen a unicorn?
Besides this groovy little unicorn? No, man. Try the **meditation** tent though.
...A unicorn? Yeah, it was unreal! We were meditating this morning and suddenly a rainbow-colored unicorn was floating in the sky like a cloud! It's the power of meditation, you know?
Sure, okay... Thanks...
MEDITATION TENT

meditation: the act of quiet concentration in order to gain spiritual awareness

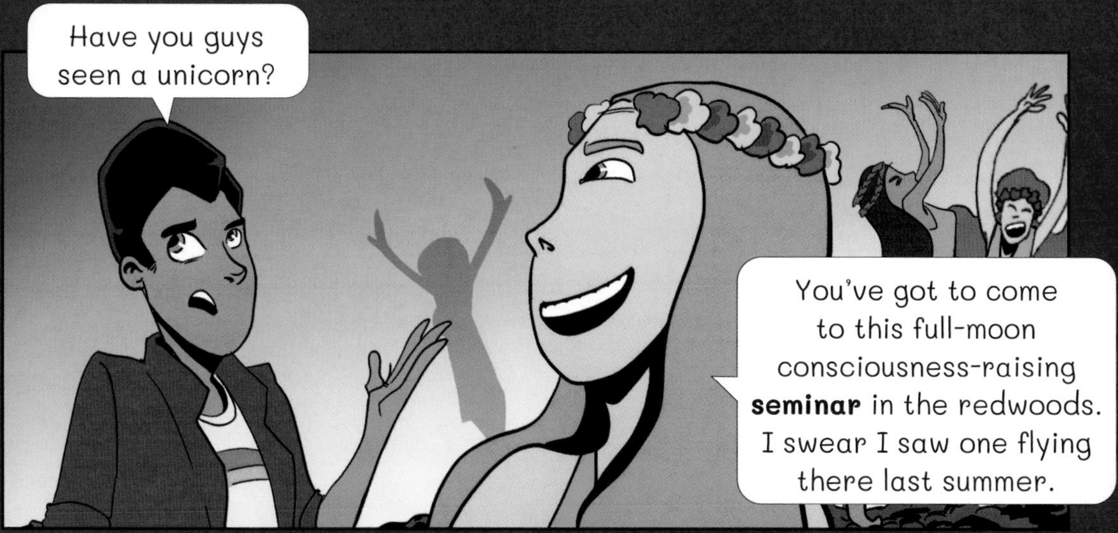

Have you guys seen a unicorn?
You've got to come to this full-moon consciousness-raising **seminar** in the redwoods. I swear I saw one flying there last summer.

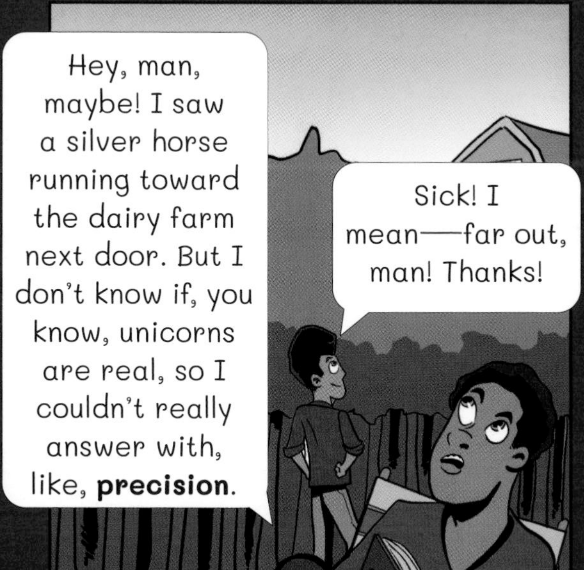

Hey, man, maybe! I saw a silver horse running toward the dairy farm next door. But I don't know if, you know, unicorns are real, so I couldn't really answer with, like, **precision**.
Sick! I mean—far out, man! Thanks!

"Consciousness raising" was a form of community activism that started in the late 1960s. Groups would meet to talk about issues like sexism, to raise awareness.

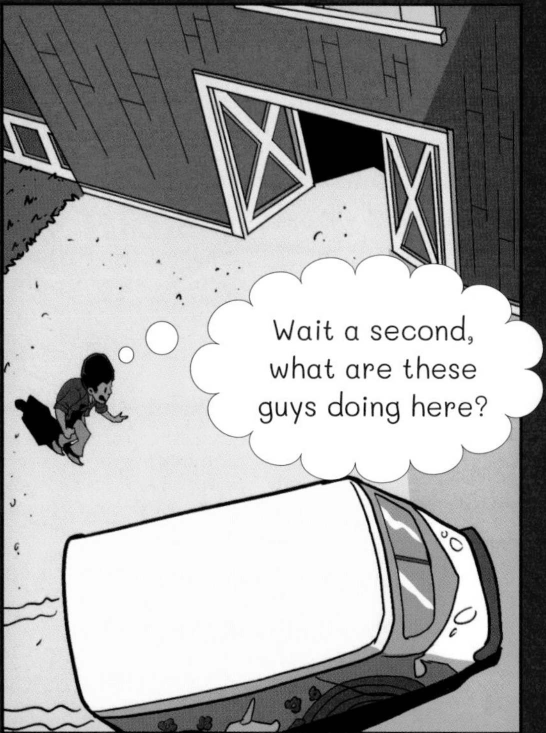

Wait a second, what are these guys doing here?

seminar: a conference or class

precision: the quality of being exact

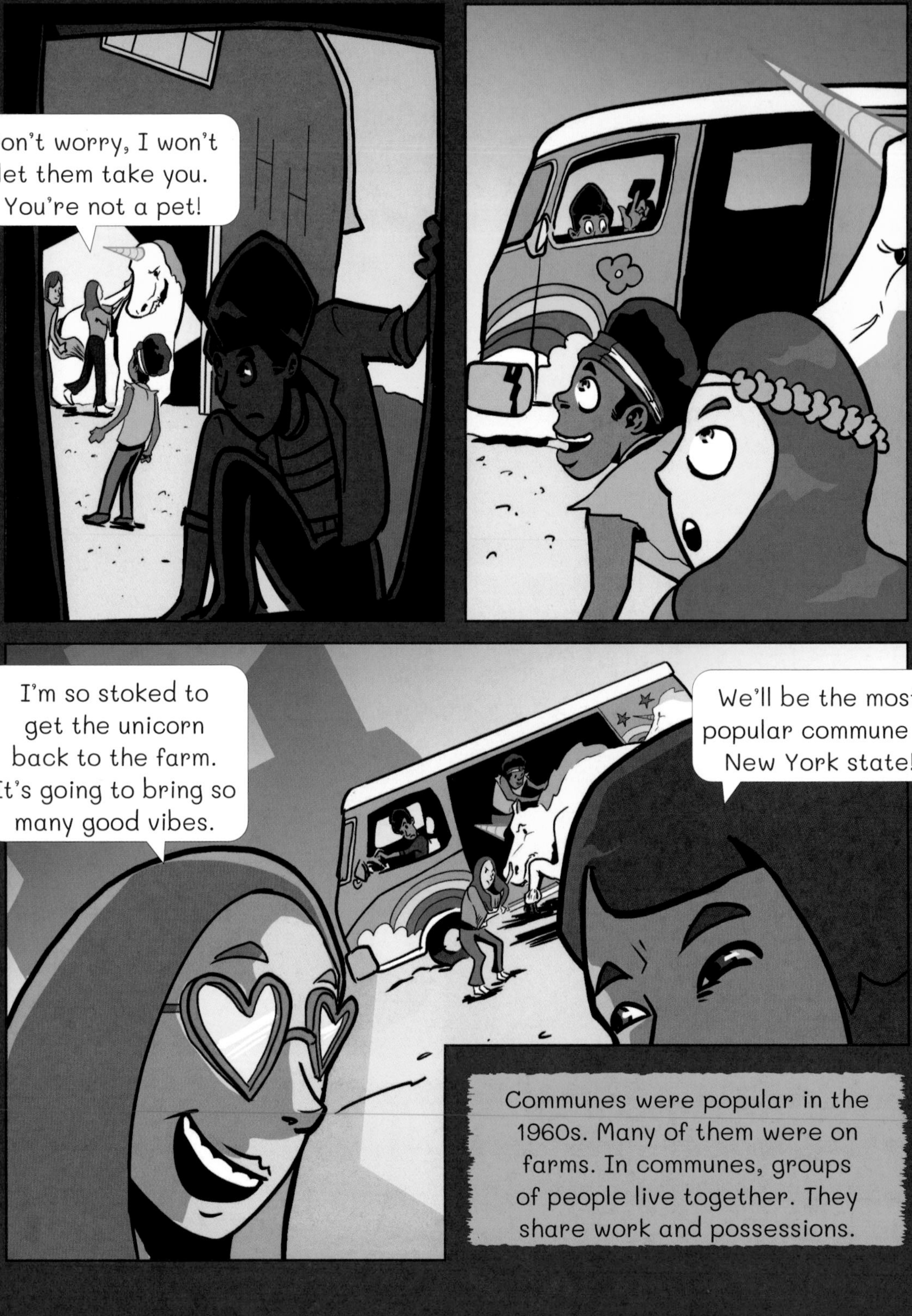
Don't worry, I won't let them take you. You're not a pet!
I'm so stoked to get the unicorn back to the farm. It's going to bring so many good vibes.
We'll be the most popular commune in New York state!
Communes were popular in the 1960s. Many of them were on farms. In communes, groups of people live together. They share work and possessions.

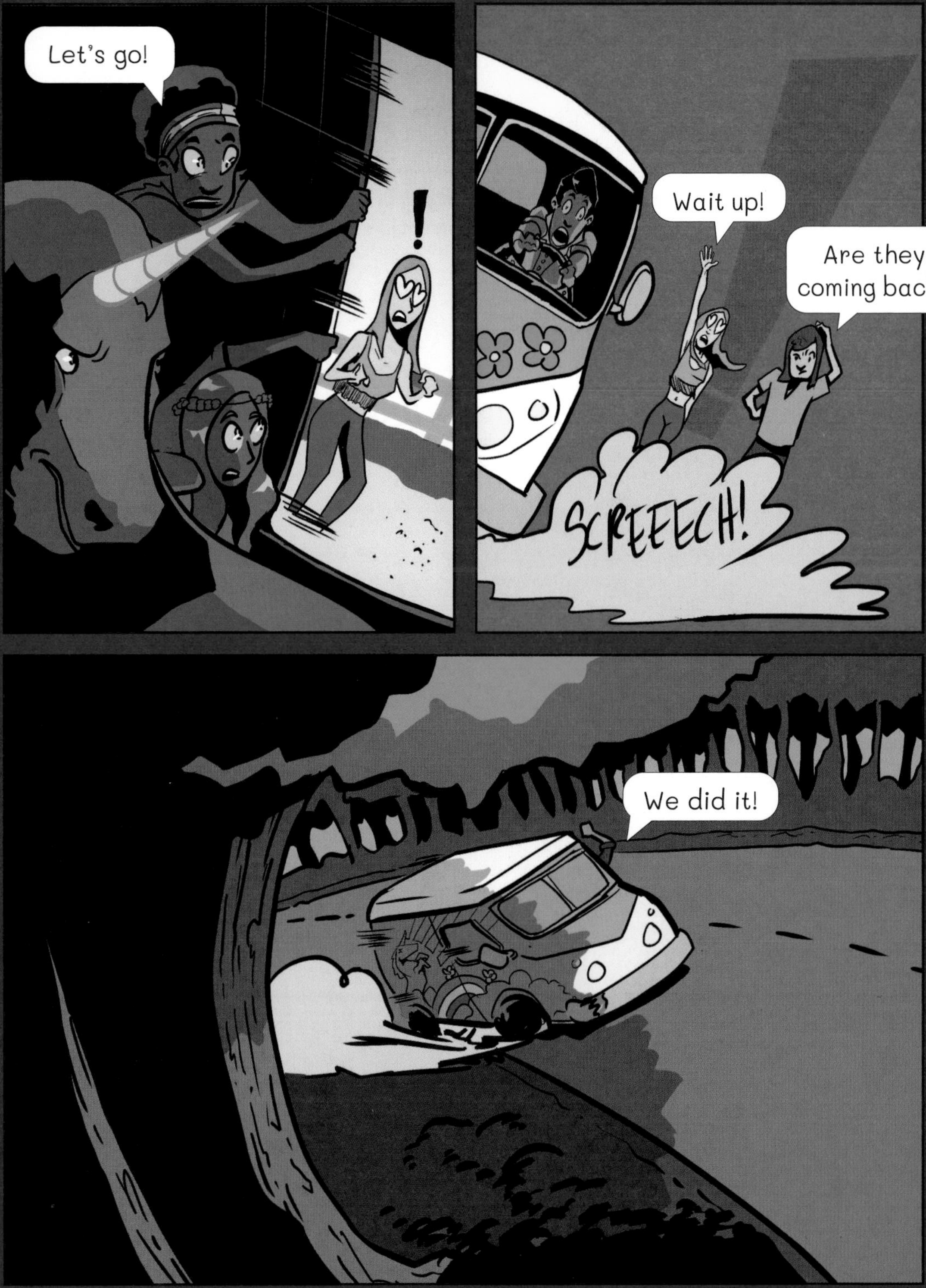
Let's go!
!
Wait up!
Are they coming back?
SCREEECH!
We did it!

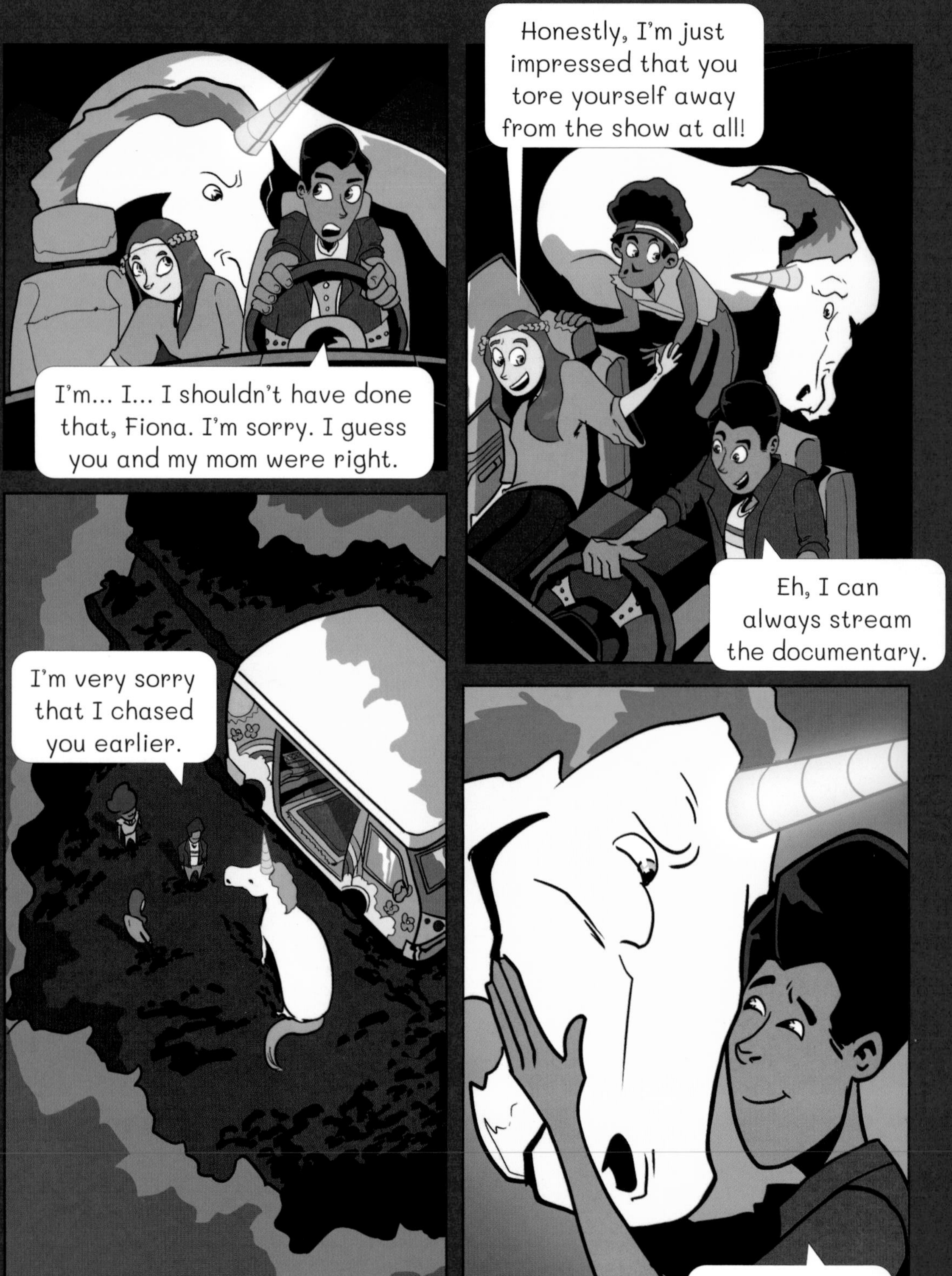
I'm... I... I shouldn't have done that, Fiona. I'm sorry. I guess you and my mom were right.
Honestly, I'm just impressed that you tore yourself away from the show at all!
Eh, I can always stream the documentary.
I'm very sorry that I chased you earlier.
Wow, he's so beautiful!

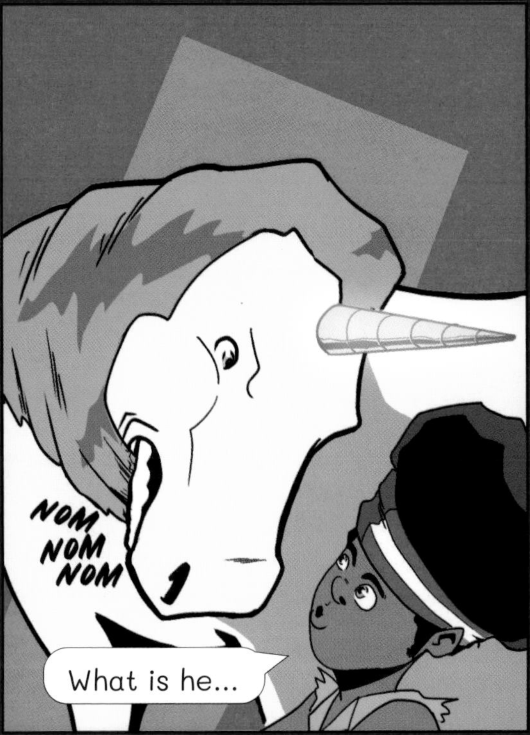
NOM NOM NOM
What is he...

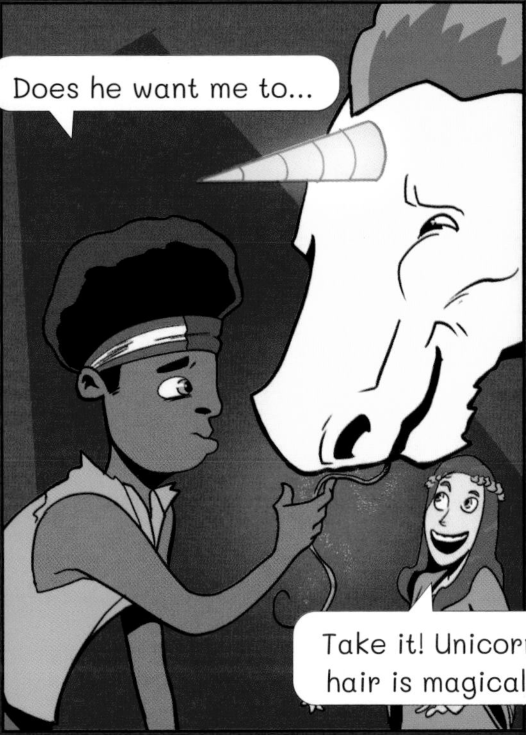
Does he want me to...
Take it! Unicorn hair is magical.

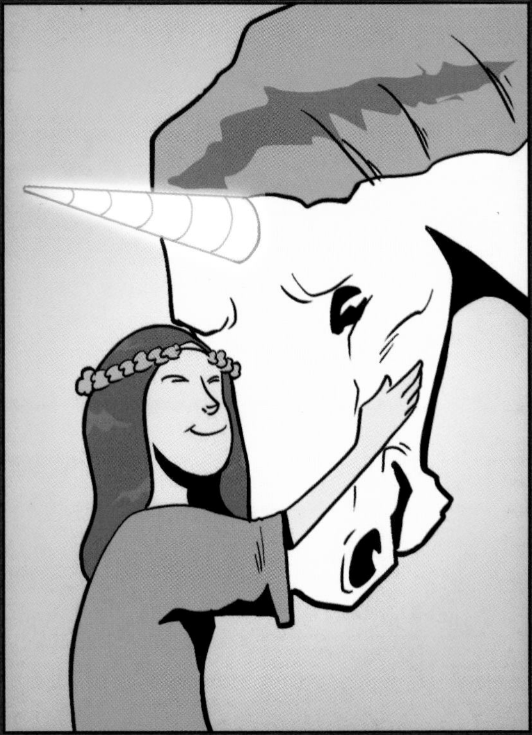

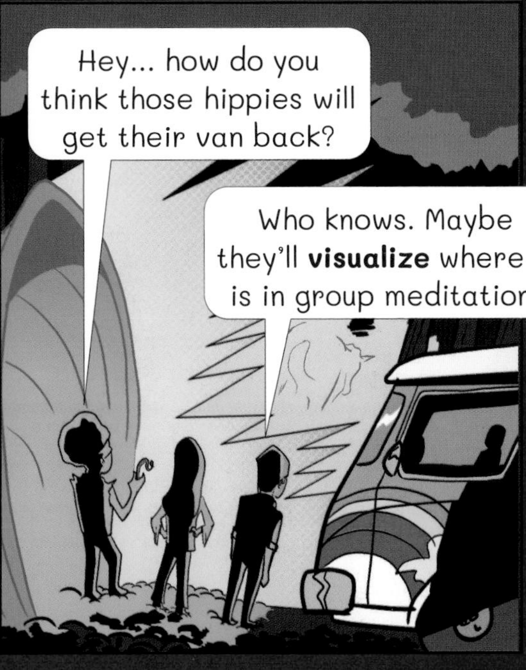
Hey... how do you think those hippies will get their van back?
Who knows. Maybe they'll **visualize** where it is in group meditation.

visualize: to form a mental image

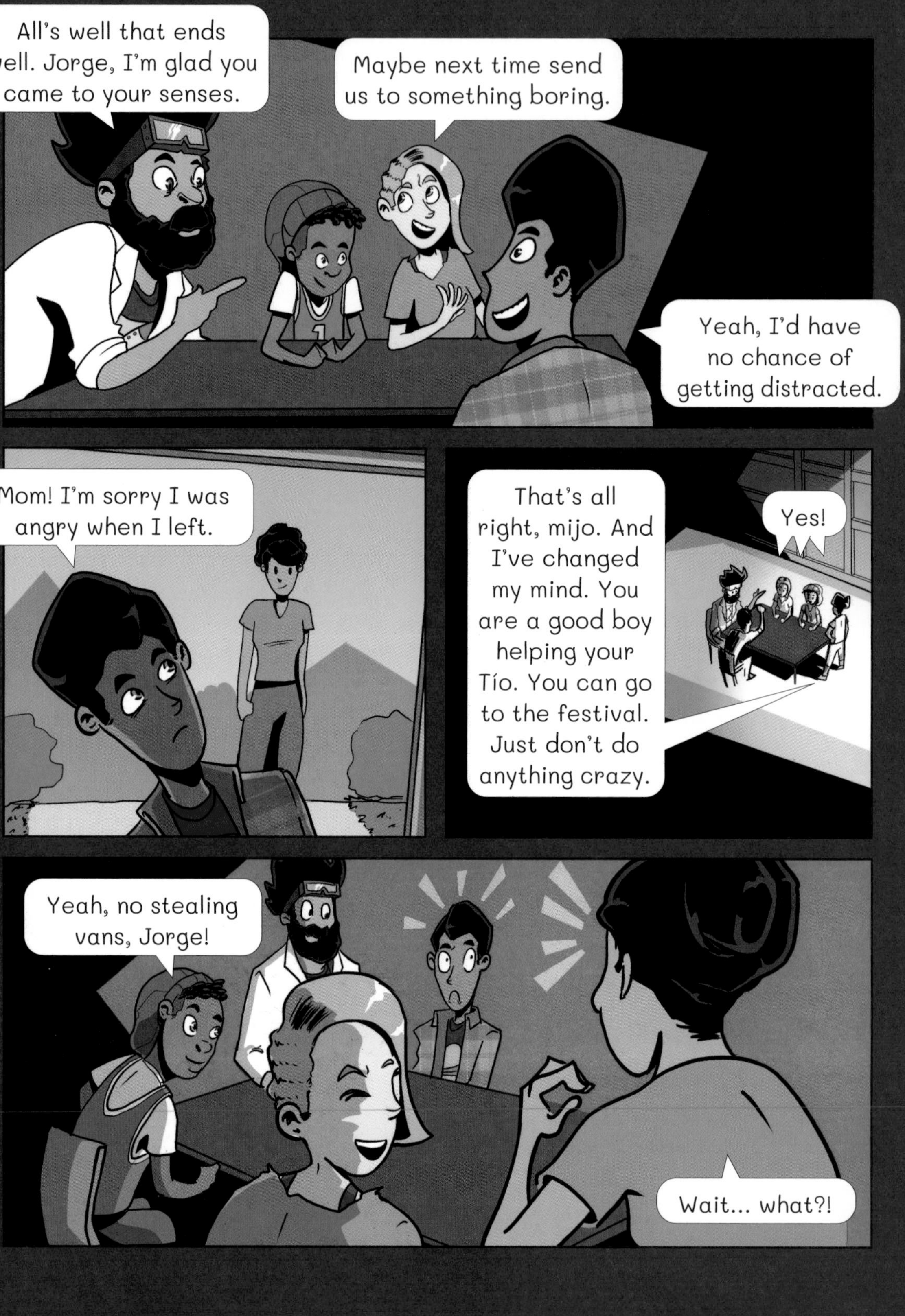
All's well that ends well. Jorge, I'm glad you came to your senses.
Maybe next time send us to something boring.
Yeah, I'd have no chance of getting distracted.
Mom! I'm sorry I was angry when I left.
That's all right, mijo. And I've changed my mind. You are a good boy helping your Tío. You can go to the festival. Just don't do anything crazy.
Yes!
Yeah, no stealing vans, Jorge!
Wait... what?!

SURVIVAL TIPS

Unicorns are difficult to find, and even more difficult to approach. But finding one is not impossible.

* They usually live in forests.

* They want to stay hidden.

* You should always ask permission to approach a unicorn. It must agree to let you come near.

Unicorns are very gentle, but they are also suspicious of humans. They will try to defend themselves. You should make sure you do not seem like a threat.

* Do not look a unicorn in the eyes.

* Don't run toward a unicorn when you are facing it. It will think you are attacking.

* Don't turn your back to unicorns. Walk calmly around them.

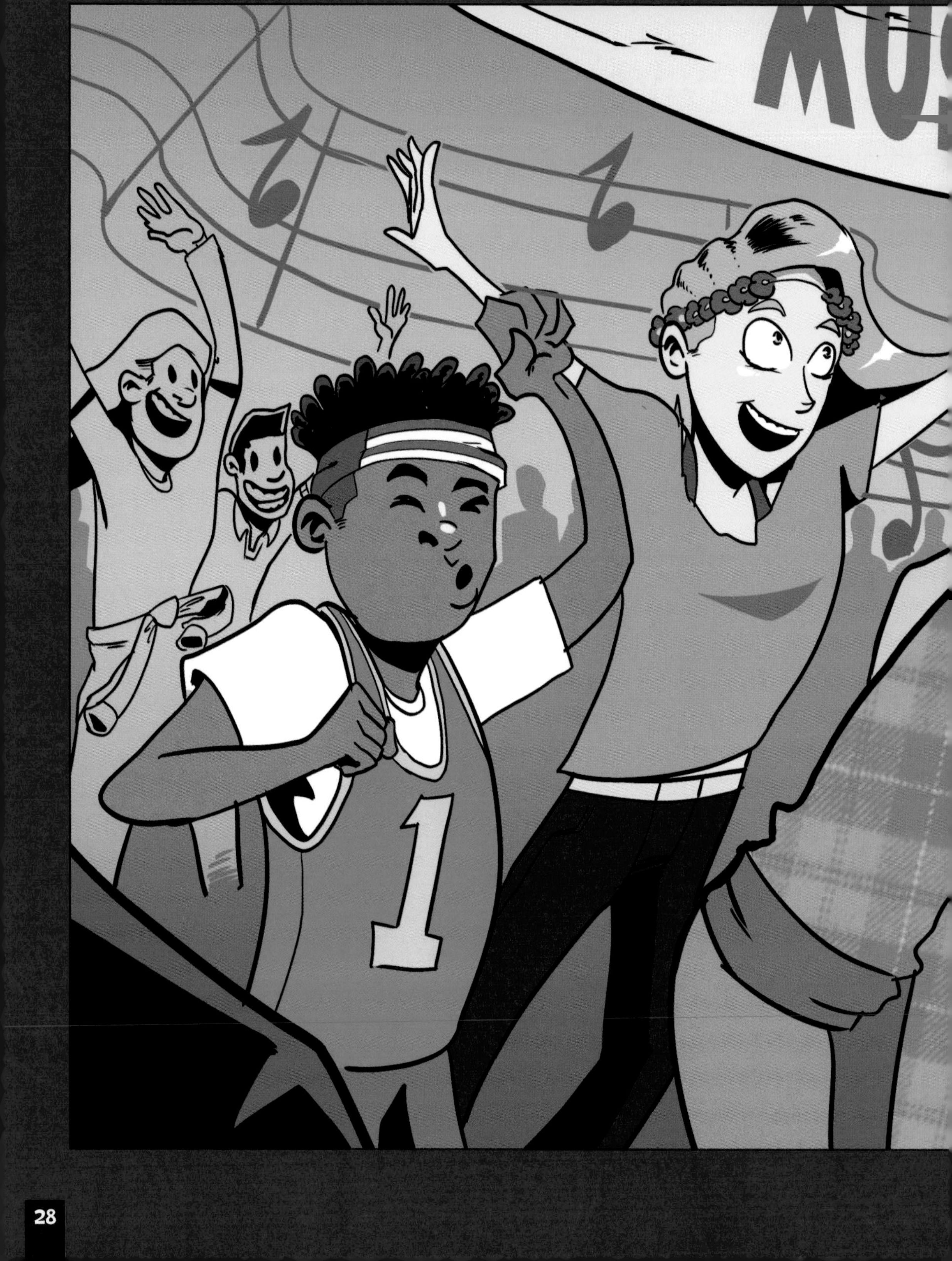
1

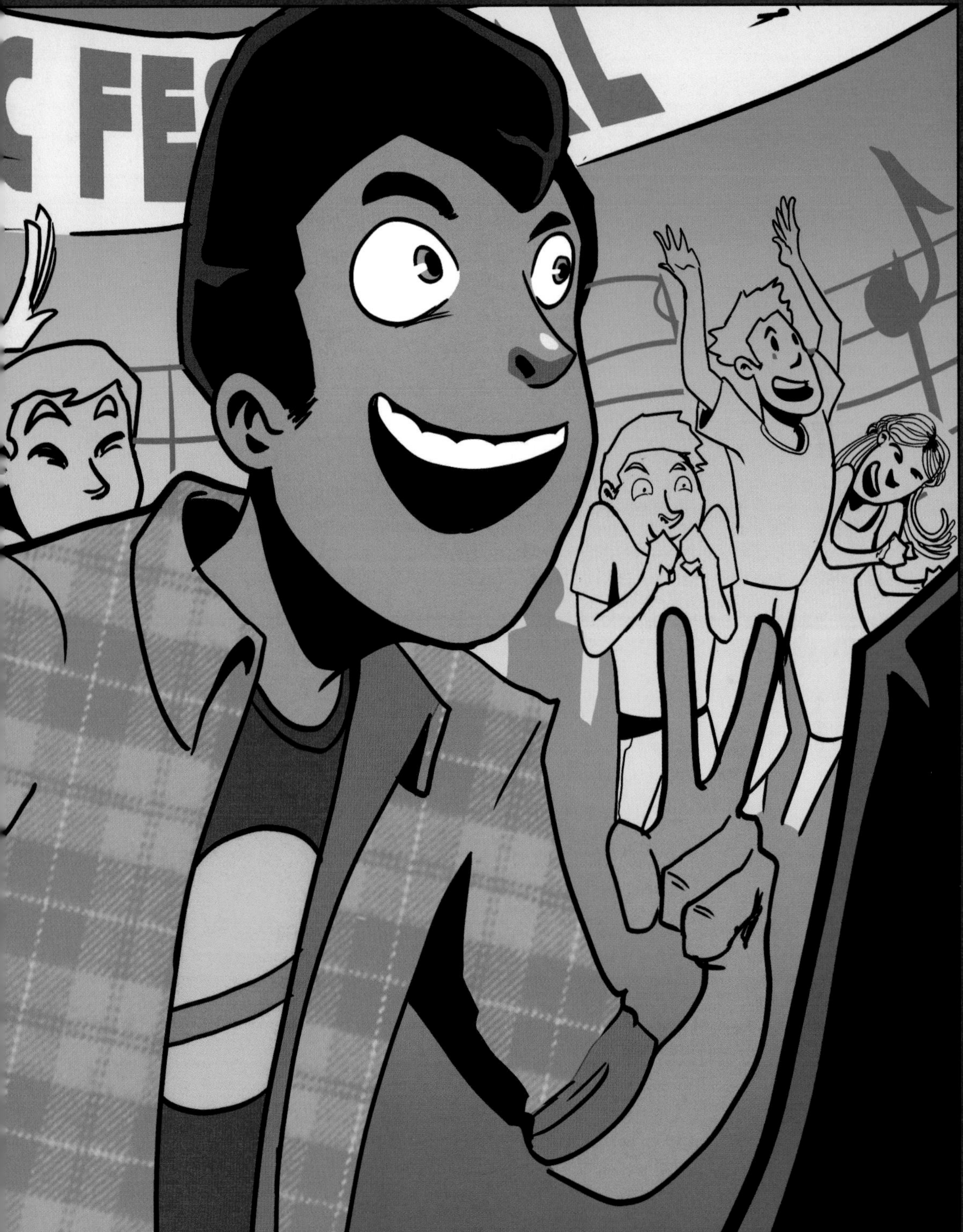

BECOME A FASHION DESIGNER

Clothing was a major defining factor in the 1960s. Some of the styles that were popular during the 60s are still popular today. Fashion designers are inventive artists. It's your turn to be a fashion designer.

Materials:

* Several sheets of paper
* Pencils for sketching
* Markers or crayons for adding color

Instructions:

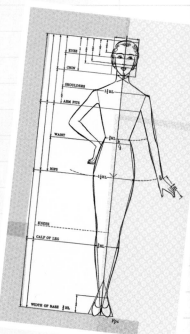

1. Choose one article of clothing to design. Sketch out a simple version of that item.
2. Use your imagination to think about how you would change it. How can you make this piece of clothing stand out?
3. If you get stuck, think about something that can inspire you. Maybe you could design something for your favorite book or movie.
4. Once you sketch out the outline, use markers and crayons to add color and texture. What will your piece of clothing feel like when it's being worn?

EYES
CHIN
SHOULDERS
ARM PITS
WAIST
HIPS
KNEES
CALF OF LEG
WIDTH OF BASE

However you design it, it will be uniquely yours!

LEARN MORE

BOOKS

Holub, Joan. *What Was Woodstock?* New York, NY: Grosset & Dunlap, 2016.

Sandling, Molly M. and Kimberley L. Chandler. *Exploring America in the 1960s: Our Voices Will Be Heard.* Waco, TX: Prufrock Press, 2014.

WEBSITES

Britannica Kids—Counterculture
https://kids.britannica.com/students/article/counterculture/310847

Luman Learning—Introduction to the Sixties
https://courses.lumenlearning.com/ushistory2americanyawp/chapter/the-sixties-2

U.S. History—Flower Power
https://www.ushistory.org/us/57h.asp

THE MONSTER HUNTER TEAM

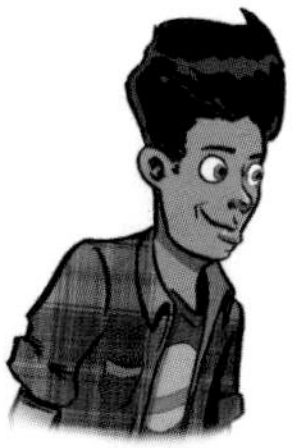

JORGE
TÍO HECTOR'S NEPHEW, JORGE, LOVES MUSIC. AT 16 HE IS ONE OF THE OLDEST MONSTER HUNTERS AND LEADER OF THE GROUP.

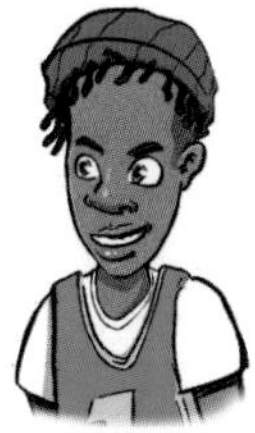

MARCUS
MARCUS IS 14 AND IS WISE BEYOND HIS YEARS. HE IS A PROBLEM SOLVER, OFTEN GETTING THE GROUP OUT OF STICKY SITUATIONS.

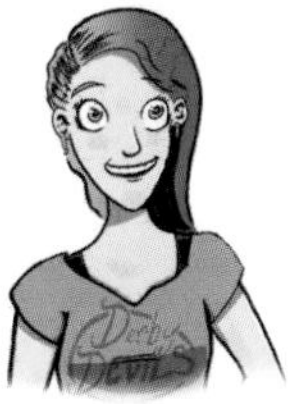

FIONA
FIONA IS FIERCE AND PROTECTIVE. AT 16 SHE IS A ROLLER DERBY CHAMPION AND IS ONE OF JORGE'S CLOSEST FRIENDS.

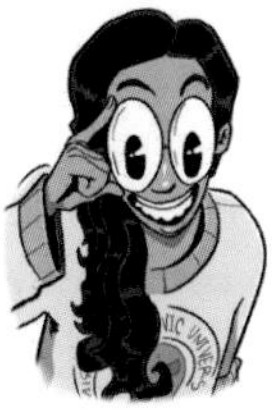

ELENA
ELENA IS JORGE'S LITTLE SISTER AND TÍO HECTOR'S NIECE. AT 14, SHE IS THE HEART AND SOUL OF THE GROUP. ELENA IS KIND, THOUGHTFUL, AND SINCERE.

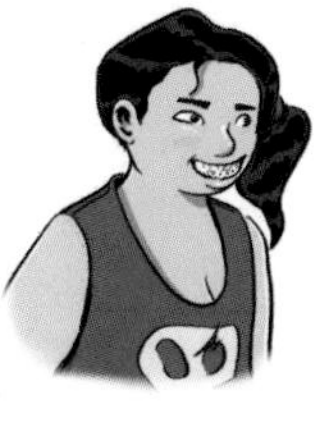

AMY
AMY IS 15. SHE LOVES BOOKS AND HISTORY. AMY AND ELENA SPEND ALMOST EVERY WEEKEND TOGETHER. THEY ARE ATTACHED AT THE HIP.

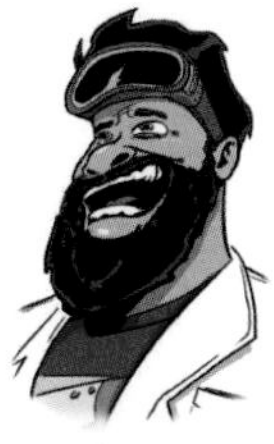

TÍO HECTOR
JORGE AND ELENA'S TÍO IS THE MASTERMIND BEHIND THE MONSTER HUNTERS. HIS TIME TRAVEL MACHINE MAKES IT ALL POSSIBLE.

GLOSSARY

agitated (A-jih-tay-ted) in a state of heightened activity

civil rights (SIH-vul RAITS) citizens' rights to freedom and equality

conformist (kun-FOR-mist) clining to accepted rules and behaviors

conservative (kun-SER-vuh-tiv) traditional

draft (DRAFT) the act of selecting people for mandatory military service

immortal (im-MOR-tul) able to live forever

legendary (LEH-jen-dary) famous

meditation (meh-dih-TAY-shun) the act of quiet concentration in order to gain spiritual awareness

mijo (MEE-hoh) "my son" in Spanish

precision (pree-SIH-zhun) the quality of being exact

seminar (SEH-mih-nahr) a conference or class

tío (TEE-oh) "uncle" in Spanish

visualize (VIH-zhoo-uh-laiz) to form a mental image

INDEX